MW00882555

Also by Gregory Brad Cutler

WHEN I AM OVERWHELMED
How to Handle Life at Its Most Intense Moments

WE DON'T ALWAYS
GET IT RIGHT THE FIRST TIME
Lessons for the Next Generation

THE PROBLEM WITH BELIEVING GOD
A Personal Guide to Increase Your Faith

WHO WE ONCE WERE

THOUGHTS KEEP FLOWING:
If You Were to Ask Me What I'm Thinking

IF WORDS COULD SPEAK:
When I can't find the words to say...

For more information visit:
www.gbcutler.com

Billboards to Better

366 Daily Sources of Motivation and Inspiration along the Highway of Life

Gregory Brad Cutler, J.D.

authorHOUSE®

AuthorHouse™
1663 Liberty Drive
Bloomington, IN 47403
www.authorhouse.com
Phone: 1 (800) 839-8640

Published by AuthorHouse 06/16/2020

ISBN: 978-1-7283-6450-6 (sc)
ISBN: 978-1-7283-6449-0 (e)

Library of Congress Control Number: 2020910773

Print information available on the last page.

Any people depicted in stock imagery provided by Getty Images are models, and such images are being used for illustrative purposes only. Certain stock imagery © Getty Images.

This book is printed on acid-free paper.

Because of the dynamic nature of the Internet, any web addresses or links contained in this book may have changed since publication and may no longer be valid. The views expressed in this work are solely those of the author and do not necessarily reflect the views of the publisher, and the publisher hereby disclaims any responsibility for them.

Scripture quotations marked KJV are from the Holy Bible, King James Version (Authorized Version). First published in 1611. Quoted from the KJV Classic Reference Bible, Copyright © 1983 by The Zondervan Corporation.

Dedication

To my mother:
Annie Elizabeth Boone Cutler

Somewhere in God's plan, He decided that you would be my mother. That single action convinces me that God's plan is perfect.

Acknowledgments

Juan Sellars and Devyn Phelps Clements,
I am eternally grateful.

To everyone who has ever joined
me on the highway of life

To everyone who embraces me as a part of humanity

To everyone who strives to become better

To everyone who has ever given me a platform

To everyone who has ever prayed for me

To everyone who has ever followed me

To everyone who has ever led me

To members of the GBC Virtual Book Club

To friends and followers of "Let's Talk to Cutler"

… THANK YOU!

Note from the Author

Imagine yourself - during a time when there was no GPS - driving along a highway without any signs or billboards. How would you locate the people and the places that are vital to your journey? How would you know whether or not you should keep going? How would you find the rest areas? How would you know when to exit?

Each day is a new day along the highway that we call "life" where we are fortunate to have signs and billboards. However, it does us no good if we don't read them. We pass by countless billboards, some that we sometimes miss because of the metaphoric traffic, the horns blowing, the distractions in our own cars, or the inappropriate speed at which we are travelling. Consider the number of times when we ignore the signs. Ignoring the signs make for a journey most miserable, but if we pay attention to the signs, the journey is made all the more pleasant.

The highway of life is fraught with potholes, accidents, detours, traffic jams, and sometimes closures that can make our journey quite challenging. We have no assurance or guarantee of a trouble-free journey, but even if the road conditions are bad, the journey can still be good as long as we don't ignore the signs. Some billboards offer motivation, inspiration, instruction, hope, or information. Some make us laugh; some make us smile; some make us angry; some make us think; and some have no effect at all.

This book provides us with daily billboards that not only motivate and inspire, but they challenge us so that when we reach our destination, we can emerge from our vehicles, having been made "BETTER" for the journey.

Pay attention to the billboards! And for those that you miss, here are 366 that you can always have with you. Enjoy the trip!

Preface

"God's Perfect Plan for My Life"

God's plan for my life is perfect,
and it's unfolding every day.
Sometimes, I'm crushed by the weight of it,
broken by the strength of it, and
bent by the responsibility of it;
but it's perfect.

I'm healed by the grace of it,
made whole by the hope of it, and
made new by the mercy of it.

It crushes my soul,
breaks my heart, and
bends my knees.

But it strengthens my hands,
steadies my feet, and
sharpens my focus.

God's plan is truly perfect.

Over the past few years of preaching sermons, teaching lessons, and engaging in conversations; I have shared what I believe to be phrases and clauses that were given to me by God's divine inspiration. In this compilation, I have collected and codified the words of my voice so that they can now be shared with the world.

If you are not willing to be critiqued by others, you're not improving yourself; you're just recycling yourself.

Children are just as
human as adults;
and they too deserve
respect. Please handle
them with care.

Have a party twice a
day: at the beginning
of the day because you
get to SEE it; and at the
end of the day because
you SURVIVED it.
You are a SEER and a
SURVIVOR.

Stop treating the CASUALTIES of war as if they are the CAUSES of war.

People who mistreat you are used by the devil. The devil is the CAUSE, so stop fighting with people. Your fight is NOT against flesh and blood. Pray for your neighbors – the good ones and the not-so-good ones.

You can't be a miracle and a mistake at the same time.

Stop bragging about telling the truth while lying about being transparent.

Just because you tell the truth, that doesn't mean you're being transparent. Truth is the veracity of the part of the story that you choose to disclose. Transparency is the veracity of the whole story, with full disclosure. When you purposefully tell the truth but still not tell the whole story, that's called manipulation.

People don't spend half
as much time thinking
about you – as you
spend thinking about
what they think of you.

Don't give people that much power over you. Stop wasting mental energy.

Don't let your "yes" to people force you to say "no" to God.

Instead of praying to
INFORM God, pray
to INVITE God. Don't
just tell Him ABOUT
your situation, but ask
Him to come INTO
your situation.

Sometimes we need
to spend MORE time
talking TO PEOPLE
who spend LESS
time talking ABOUT
PEOPLE. Choose better
conversation partners.

You don't need perfect vision to see a favorable future.

> Even if it doesn't come FROM God, it has to come THROUGH God. Nothing that comes to harm you is going to catch God by surprise.

Missiles can be diverted. Wars can be averted. Schemes can be subverted. NONE of them catches God by surprise. The weapon might form, but trust that God will "HALT or HIDE." If He doesn't halt the weapon, He will hide you from it. "For in the time in trouble he shall hide me…" (Psalm 27:5).

> If you're going to
> welcome God in, you
> can't give Him a check-
> out date.

The heart is the altar where we invite God to abide. Make sure your altar is a dwelling place and not just for occasional visitation.

Punctuate your life
properly. What you're
going through today
is not a "period."
It's just a "comma."
Commas have
something fulfilling
and completing on the
other side.

Suffering and trouble are never meant
to be the final plan. They are just commas.
Punctuate every trial with a comma, and have
hope because of what's on the other side.

January 15

Quite often we bind
ourselves by the very
boundaries that we've
drawn for others.

15

Unless you have people
who doubt you, deny
you, and betray you;
you won't know for
sure that you have any
who love you.

I'd rather forget to sin,
than to sin and forget.

Truth is either relative
or absolute; but then
there's a lie.

> Don't ever let your fingers do the job that your mouth was meant to do.

In a day when the cost of the phone call is no longer a factor, we've opted not to call. Instead, we send text messages, emails, and social media posts. There has never been a substitute for hearing the voice, yet somehow, we have managed to evolve into a society that no longer feels the need to talk to people personally.

Fellowship is not easily
achieved when you're
in the boat alone.

Just because life is
shifting the gears,
that doesn't mean that
God is not holding the
steering wheel.

God shakes, but He
cannot be shaken; God
moves, but He cannot
be moved. He is the
unmoved mover and
the unshaken shaker.

Sometimes God allows things to seem unstable, but He is not moved by life. He is neither agitated by conditions nor intimidated by circumstances.

Boldness is just as much about knowing when to keep silent as knowing when to speak.

I don't worry about not knowing the plan of God, as long as I know the God of the plan.

It's nice to be IN their corner, but it's better to BE their corner!

Sometimes struggles last a long time so that you can get a good look at what God is carrying you through.

A good testimony will
keep you delivered and
the enemy defeated.

Be careful about asking
God to do to other
people what you don't
want him to do to you!

If you don't want God to shut your mouth, you might want to reconsider your request.

When you are sharing the gospel, remember that you're just delivering the mail. You didn't write the letter, and you're not the sender.

When God speaks, He resets the calendar of your life. Everything that happened before He spoke really doesn't matter. He knows how to make all things new.

When God spoke to Moses and Aaron in Exodus 12:1-2, He told them that the month wherein He was speaking "shall be the first month of the year to you."

God deserves so
much more than the
leftovers of our lives.
He's gracious enough
to accept them, but
He deserves so much
more.

Always be ready to receive what God is ready to send.

It is more than rhetoric to suggest that sometimes we must hearken unto the voice of God, or the leading of the Spirit, so that we can be prepared to receive the blessings that He sends. When God was preparing the children of Israel for their deliverance from Egyptian bondage, He gave specific instructions concerning the Passover. In Exodus 12:11, God was basically telling the Israelites to eat, be dressed, and be prepared for deliverance.

You don't need the Red
Sea to have a "Red Sea
experience." God will
show up and make
the enemy think twice
about pursuing you.

Never forget your personal "Red Sea
experiences." Don't ever let life get you so far
down that you forget how God brought you
out; how He healed you; how He made a way;
how He saved you; how He opened doors;
how He blessed your family. Don't forget.
And when you remember, celebrate. And just
before you forget, celebrate again!

Whenever you meet a perfect person, turn away and run as fast as possible.

Faith is not just
BELIEF IN – but it's
DEPENDABILITY
ON – God's capacity to
handle it!

The true enemy of faith - and the essence
of sin – is believing that we can do it
without God.

If you don't understand
God's promises,
you will never
fully appreciate His
provisions.

> # When you stand with God, He won't let you sit alone in shame.

The woman who washed the feet of Jesus with her tears and dried them with her hair was a sinner and she knew it. She was not there to discuss doctrine or theology. She wasn't there to challenge Jesus to a debate. She was there to seek forgiveness the best way she could. She kissed his feet and anointed them with ointment from her alabaster box (Luke 7:37-38). And she wept profusely. Ultimately, Jesus told the woman: "Thy faith hath saved thee; go in peace" (Luke 7:50).

Don't mishandle the sinner while trying to handle the sin. Do what you do in the "spirit of meekness" (Galatians 6:1).

For every wrong turn
on the road of life,
there is a roadmap to
recovery.

"If my people, which are called by my name, shall humble themselves, and pray, and seek my face, and turn from their wicked ways; then will I hear from heaven, and will forgive their sin, and will heal their land" (2 Chronicles 7:14).

Don't get stuck when
God says "no;" just
rejoice when He says
"yes."

Get out of God's way;
He knows what He's
doing; and He knows
where He's going.

We are the reward that
Jesus saw through all
of His suffering. May
we NEVER cause Him
to regret His decision.

Discipline is not about COMFORT; it's about CHARACTER. God disciplines and chastises us because He loves us. Discipline does not necessarily feel good, but it works out for our good.

If we are sitting in heavenly places with Christ Jesus, we should be able to see things from God's point of view.

Good works don't always lead; quite often they follow.

> Stop engaging in self-destructive behavior and then pretending that you're not committing suicide.

When we choke our dreams, hopes, and ambitions; we commit suicide. When we don't eat properly or rest well, we commit suicide. When we live under the weight of stress and anxiety – instead of casting our anxieties, fears, and tears at the altar – we commit suicide. When we forfeit the opportunity to live with Christ, we live WITHOUT Him, and we commit suicide.

Just because we're not following, that doesn't mean God is not leading.

"He leadeth me in the paths of righteousness…" (Psalm 23:3). God is committed to leading us, but the choice to follow is ours. Let's choose wisely.

When you wake up, decide right then and there that you are going to have a good day. Make a decision to be happy.

"This is day which the Lord hath made; we will rejoice and be glad in it" (Psalm 118:24).

> The brevity of people's
> presence in your
> life doesn't lessen
> the impact that God
> intended them to have.

Learn to let go of the people and things that were intended to be in your life short-term. Don't get upset because relationships or circumstances don't last forever. It just might be God's plan for them to have a brief stay. After Phillip led the Ethiopian eunuch to Christ, the Bible says that Phillip was taken away and seen no more by the Eunuch (Acts 8:39).

Make a decision to
start believing God,
even when you don't
understand Him.
Don't insult God by
disbelieving what He
called you to be.

Relationships, like bridges, have to be carefully constructed and consistently maintained.

Give your voice
permission to sing,
your heart permission
to love, your mind
permission to dream,
and your soul
permission to soar.

> My cleansing is of no
> benefit if I constantly
> bathe in muddy water.

Many times the duration of our success
is temporary and short-lived because our
perspective of success is short-sighted and
myopic. Strive for success that encompasses
everything includes not only you but your
surroundings as well.

Stop expecting God to agree with you, when you won't even unite with Him.

Don't let people
contaminate the things
that God expects you
to sanctify.

Guard your hopes and dreams with
everything within you. Blessings and miracles
come from God. Handle them well.

God's redemption plan is not like man's repayment plan. Redemption doesn't come in installments.

God keeps two things:
His promise and His
people.

One person's place
of suffering could be
another person's place
of salvation.

In the same city where Paul was stoned, a crippled man was healed. (Acts 14).

If you trust God BEFORE the struggle, you can expect to hear Him DURING the struggle.

It's easier than you may know to become the thing that you despise.

When the rich man turned up his nose at Lazarus because he was poor and needy, he failed to see that he himself immediately became needy ... of forgiveness, mercy, and an attitude adjustment.

He got the stripes, but I got the healing.

God consciously
decided … to let you
live. Think about that.
Then say, "Thanks."

If you confess it, God
will confront it. Have
the energy to speak
your truth; God's got
the power to make it
bless you.

Every empty area in
your life is nothing
more than another
opportunity for God to
fill you up!

Because God promised
you a future, He covers
you with favor.

To some people, we may look like our past (or even our present), but God speaks to the future within.

Don't treat God like
a sports athlete; don't
change your opinions
about Him based on
His performance.

What if God handled
us the same way that
we handle him?

Because of grace,
we survived on
battlegrounds where
we should have died.

When your problem says "pit," let your praise say "palace." God loves you too much to leave you in a pit.

When we are intimidated by the thing that we possess, then the thing that we possess has begun to possess us.

Embrace your originality and authenticity.

Don't end up crucifying what you thought you were critiquing.

Be careful not to kill the things that came to give you life - just because they challenge you to become better. Jesus came to bring life, but the crowd wanted to kill him.

Let your life reflect
what your faith
declares.

If you believe it, then act on the thing that
you believe. Give your faith a body to work
with.

> You will never optimize
> the things that are
> worth living for, until
> you identify the things
> in your life that are
> worth dying for.

You will never fully live in peace until peace becomes something worth dying for. You will never have your greatest success unless victory is worth dying for.

All you need is an audience of one! Keep telling your story and singing your song, even if no one seems to be listening.

A believer's
identification card
will never work in the
wallet of a counterfeit.

A counterfeit can never duplicate your true essence or the totality of what defines and describes you as a child of God, whether it's your name, the way you talk, the way you smile, or the way you treat people.

It's much more important to have a new life than a new start.

Just because you get a new start, that doesn't mean you get new tools; so you're prone to make some of the same mistakes. However, with a new life, God will add new weapons to your arsenal and new benefits to your compensation package. When Jesus healed the ten lepers in Luke 17, only one of them turned back to give thanks and glorify God. Only one fell at His feet in a posture of worship to give thanks (Luke 17:15-16). And ultimately, because of his faith, his worship, and his gratitude; he didn't get just a new start. He got a new life.

Even if the enemy puts
you in it, God knows
how to get you out of
it. God will consume
the enemies of your
life with the same fires,
traps, and pitfalls that
were set for you.

We often read about the three Hebrew
boys who were thrown in the fiery furnace –
and survived; but we forget that these "most
mighty men" who threw them into the
furnace were themselves consumed by the
flames of the fire (Daniel 3:22).

Be honest with God; after all, He already knows.

What your faith IN
God might not do, your
friendship WITH God
will. If Abraham can
be called the "Friend
of God" (James 2:23),
then so can you.

> There are no guarantees that God's promises will come without pain.

God promised – and gave – Abraham a son named Isaac, but He told Abraham to offer the son as a burnt offering on the mountain (Genesis 22:1-3). Although God prepared a substitute sacrifice instead of Isaac, we have no guarantees that some of the things that God promised us will not die and cause us grief and heartache. But just because it dies, that doesn't mean that it was no less a promise, delivered by the hands of God.

Don't expect God to be agreeable, if you're not going to be available!

Your life is going to
testify for you, whether
you want it to or not.

Even when you can't
tell it all, at least tell
enough.

John, the beloved apostle, realized that Jesus had done so many wonderful things that the world couldn't contain enough books to tell it all (John 21:23). And although John couldn't tell it all, he told enough … to lead us into a relationship with Christ.

Walk as one who has been called, not as one who has been condemned.

Be very careful with trying to make an assessment about the presence of God in the lives of other people.

Consider an egg; you can't see what God is doing inside that shell.

Stay out of the hell
that others create for
themselves; believers
are called to sit in
heavenly places.

The beggar named Lazarus was not a
part of the hellish demise that the rich man
created for himself (Luke 16:19-24).

I would rather do
without it down here,
if it's going to keep me
from going up there.

Stop looking FOR God,
and look AT God.
Behold the beauty of
His splendor and the
wonder of His majesty.

Just look around and see him; "the whole earth is full of His glory" (Isaiah 6:3).

Our hands can't hold what God's hands can.

Out of all the things we can make, we still can't make a world.

I would rather
give God an UGLY
TRUTH rather than a
PRETTY LIE.

It's during the darkest moments that we have our brightest dreams.

We get our reminders during the daylight, but we had the dreams in the dark.

If you will be faithful
with the water, God
will give you the wine.

April 2

Your present weakness
doesn't begin to
compare with your
future strength.

No matter how good we are, we are better when God answers our prayer; so keep praying.

Sometimes the way
is made FOR us; but
sometimes the way is
made BY us.

Even in my brokenness, God deserves my best. Don't slack up on God just because life turns up the fire.

You don't always have to know the purpose in order to follow the plan.

God told Noah to build the ark. THEN He told him about the flood (Genesis 6:14-17).

> Today they see your shame, but tomorrow they will see your shine.

God has several tomorrow's in your life; and although people one day laughed AT you, there will be a tomorrow when they laugh WITH you! Sarah doubt God's ability to give her a child in her old age, so she walked around in the shame of never having produced a child. She even laughed at the thought of God's ability to give her a child, but when the child came forth, her laughter of skepticism changed into a laughter of joy. And Sarah declared that he would laugh and rejoice so much "that all that hear will laugh with [her]" (Genesis 21:6).

April 8

Nothing mends a
relationship like
repentance.

People can't see your
roots, but they can
always see your fruit.

Wherever I'm going
with God is better
than where I've been
without Him.

A powerful voice
is sometimes most
effective when it is
silent.

Your mouth and your
life should speak the
same language.

Sometimes our mouths lead people TO
God, but our lives lead people FROM God.
Could it be that people don't believe in God
and trust God because of the version of "God"
that they have seen in us?

God doesn't just watch
His word to perform it,
but He performs it so
WE can watch it.

There are many things
that you can spread,
but a lie shouldn't be
one of them.

What looked like shame on the cross turned into victory in the grave.

Relationships are free;
it's the maintenance
that costs.

Salvation is free, but discipleship costs.

Christ is coming, and
I'm going.

Faith is the anchor that
keeps me from drifting.

Strive to make God
proud every day!

Purpose is not what
happens when life
begins, but life is what
happens when purpose
begins.

You are never too young to walk in
purpose. Part of John's (the Baptist) purpose
was to announce the presence of Christ, and
he started doing that while in his mother's
womb. The Bible says that when the Mary
(who was pregnant with Jesus) visited her
cousin Elizabeth (who was pregnant with
John), the baby in Elizabeth's womb leaped,
and Elizabeth was filled with the Holy Ghost
(Luke 1:41).

I get excited when God is blessing my neighbor because at least He's in my community.

God's got a way of
making sure that even
if you're out of His will,
you're never out of His
reach. He knows how
to bring righteousness
to the wayward and
guidance to the lost.

What God intends
for you will find you,
even if it has to travel
through time.

God's promise has the power to penetrate through generations. God made a promise to Abraham that was manifested through the coming of Jesus Christ. His promise, like a well arched bow, strikes with precision; even if it has to pierce through generations before striking its target.

Everything is subject
to change when God
shows up. My heart
changes; my mind
changes; and my
whole life changes,
just because God …
decides to show up.

When it comes to God,
teach your children
more than a casual
acquaintance with an
occasional visitor.

You are the model of a relationship with God for your children. He trusted you with them, so be careful to demonstrate the essence of worship, the power of praise, the tenets of trust, and the necessity of respect. Teach them God!

When God wrote the plan for my life, He planned for me to win.

He knew all the miracles He would work, all the ways He would make, all the victories He would win, and all the trials He would bring me through. When He wrote the plan, He included my testimony.

> Your temptation might
> be part of God's plan.
> Don't fail the test.

If Jesus was led into the wilderness to be tempted (Matthew 4:1), then our temptations and wilderness experience might just be a part of God's plan.

Don't let your physical
desires compromise
your spiritual destiny.

Be careful about following, when the enemy is leading.

Stop trying to prove
your relationship
WITH God to people
who don't even
KNOW God.

Stay in the game; the enemy will ultimately reveal his hand.

I don't worry about God hiding things from me; I'm just glad that He hides me from things.

How high you lift
others today could
determine how high
you soar tomorrow.

If you do the right thing when it's difficult, it will become difficult to do the wrong thing when it's easy.

God is probably more interested in changing me, than He is in changing my situation.

If He changes me, I have the faith to believe that He will give me the ability to change my situation.

Believe God, simply
because God can
and because God …
simply can!

You were created to reflect the creative power of the One who creates!

Stop pushing against
the wall, and just lean
on it for a change.
Everything doesn't
come to challenge you.
Some things come to
give you rest.

If you trust God during
what looks like the
foolish times, He won't
fool you during the
trying times.

Believe in God, without the word "in." Don't just believe that He is, but believe what He says.

It is one thing to believe in the existence and capabilities of people, but it's something completely different to believe in the candor, the veracity, and the truth of what they say.

In order to kiss the
right people hello,
sometimes you've
got to kiss the wrong
people goodbye.

Be less concerned
when people try to
hurt your feelings and
more concerned when
they try to hurt your
future.

If the smilers would
stop frowning, maybe
the frowners would
start smiling.

Optimism is contagious.

May 14

God will never ask you
to walk away without
first strengthening your
legs.

Pain might last for just a little while, but resentment can last forever.

When life tries to bury
you, spread your roots
and grow.

Position and prestige
mean nothing without
principle and practice.

Death isn't the ultimate winner. We defeat death every morning we wake up; and even when I die, guess what! We're getting up. That's the hope of the believer.

I am never more
powerful than when
I am at peace because
that is when I have
conquered my greatest
foe – myself.

Surround yourself
with people who know
how stay in control,
especially when
you're not.

It's better to have one elevator that DOES
work, rather than two that don't.

You're just as strong
as the last person who
endured what you now
face.

I would rather have
opportunity knock
when I'm partially
ready; rather than have
it never knock and I'm
fully ready.

Learning to accept the
truth is sometimes like
standing naked and
allowing yourself to be
reborn.

No matter how graceful it may appear, it is a confused fish that swims in the wrong direction. Just because you're moving, that doesn't mean you're on the right course.

When you discover your path, stay on it. Otherwise, you might end up in a snare or in the mouth of a predator.

It's better to eat your cooking than your words. Think twice before you speak wickedly about somebody or try to shame them, because they might be the ones who you need to restore you one day.

Job's friends talked about him and falsely accused him, but ultimately, they need him to pray for them (Job 42:10).

God is better than
the best security
system. When He
protects, we don't have
to worry about the
enemy sneaking in or
breaking through. God
is on watch!

Never make an outsider feel like an outsider; otherwise, you risk him never becoming an insider.

God does not have a
bad memory, but it's
still okay to remind
Him of His track
record.

"Lord, thou art God, which has made
heaven, and earth, and the sea, and all that in
them is" (Acts 4:24).

When you're doing wrong, don't pull others into your mess; and when you're doing right, don't let others pull you into theirs.

Oppose opposition and resist resistance!

The message matters much more than the messenger and the methods.

June 1

The tenets of your faith
should NEVER be up
for discussion.

You can disagree about doctrine, but don't
ever argue about your faith. Contend for it;
fight for the right to have it; but never argue
about it.

> Sometimes the old thing that we already have is better than the new thing that we seek.

Stop spending so much time looking for new revelations and "new" words when Jesus spent much of his ministry reminding people of what he had already said.

Religion is good when taught, but better when lived.

Failure doesn't have to be the finale!

Peter's repeated denial of Christ was followed by cursing, swearing, and eventually by tears (Mark 14:66-72). Denying Christ was indeed a horrible thing, but Peter's sin, like ours, did not create a situation that was impossible for Christ to handle.

Always keep somebody around you who can reach Jesus for you when you don't think you can reach Him for yourself. Stay connected to people who stay connected to God.

Whether God says "yes" or "no," you still have an answer.

Sometimes the most important thing about God's answer is the fact that He answered.

When it comes to God,
you should always
expect an encounter or
an experience.

He creates a whole mood, all by Himself!

Forgiveness is not a trump card in a game of spades!

Don't hold on to forgiveness, flaunt it over people, and then dispatch it so that you can emerge as the victor of some battle where scores are kept. Release it just as quickly as you received it.

Want for yourself what
God wants for you.

God's thoughts
concerning you are not
influenced by anyone
else's opinions.

He does not require a majority vote to bless you. As Jesus was passing through Jericho (Luke 19:1-6) Zacchaeus wanted to see Him, but was too short so he climbed up a sycamore tree. Jesus saw him, told him to come down out of the tree, and told him that He was going to spend more time with him at his house. The crowd murmured and complained, but Jesus was not moved by their complaints. He came to see the lost (Luke 19:10), and He will find us, even if He has to look up in a tree.

If you can't build God a house, at least build God an altar. He doesn't require a whole lot. He'll accept the little that you have to offer.

I would rather have credibility with God rather than visibility by man.

June 13

Ungodly thinking leads
to unrighteous doing.

Stop confusing "good intentions" with "Godly pursuits."

God gets left out of a lot of good intentions.

Having the favor of God in my life does not make me BETTER than anybody else. It simply makes me as BLESSED as everybody else.

The reward of my discomfort is that I get to look like God. Every challenge that we overcome transforms us more into the likeness of God.

When God chastises us, He makes us more like Him. He chastises us so that we "might be a partaker of his holiness" (Hebrews 12:10).

Stop putting human characteristics on God, and let's put Godly characteristics on humans.

Don't kick people while they are down because their climb back up just might save your life.

The peace of God is
so powerful that it can
cause foes to become
friends (Isaiah 11:6).

There is no bedroom
near God's throne.
He never sleeps, takes
a nap, or gets tired
(Isaiah 40:28).

Every time God turns
the page in your life,
you get to show up like
a brand new character.

The creator - not the institution - was meant to be worshipped.

Two things will keep you from winning the race: sin and weight (Hebrews 12:1).

Having a relationship
with God is not a
matter of bloodline;
it's a matter of being
blood-washed.

> # There is no unrestricted access to heaven.

You don't get to just randomly walk in. There is no admission without a ticket. Get your ticket today!

The footprint of God has caused an eternal ripple effect in my life. God makes all the difference when He steps in. His footprint changes things forever.

Mary grew up in a nation that had been in captivity and with a future that was looking bleak – until God stepped in. Her cousin Elisabeth had spent most of her adult life wanting something that she couldn't have – until God stepped in. Invite God to step in!

Your purpose is connected to who you are – not what you do; therefore, purpose is fulfilled by your presence. Make sure you SHOW UP.

Sometimes we miss the opportunity to walk in purpose because we don't SHOW UP. When Mary showed up, her cousin Elisabeth was filled with the Holy Ghost (Luke 1:41). It's important to SHOW UP!

Even if you dream
in pieces, the parts
will eventually come
together. Just dream.

Stop imposing God's
requirements of you
onto other people. If
He told you what to do,
then YOU do it!

God didn't tell me that I had to pray at
5:00AM. God didn't tell me that I had to go
to the bathroom and pray at 12:00 noon. He
didn't tell me that I had to fast three days a
week. Outside of the context of corporate
worship and congregational practices, stop
imposing God's mandates for you onto others.

Make sure you
understand the
difference between
culture and covenant.
Culture is "how" I
do it, but covenant is
"why" I do it.

Walking in faith will lead you to salvation; living totally in flesh will lead you to damnation.

Agreeing is not a prerequisite to loving.

God does not always agree with us. Yet He chose to love us.

If people reject the
picture that you
are trying to paint,
perhaps it's because
your spiritual canvas
has been defiled.

As "living epistles," our responsibility is
to present an excellent crucified Christ. We
have to be careful to paint an accurate picture
by depicting the love of God. If we engage in
ungodly behavior, we defile our canvas and
skew the picture of Christ that we try to paint.

Wear the years well
and treat them as a
friend, so others may
see how good God has
been.

When you're wrong,
seek forgiveness. When
you're right, seek
humility.

July 6

Live honorably so
that when your life is
quoted, someone else is
made better.

We are living epistles, read of men (2
Corinthians 3:2).

He wouldn't promise it
if He couldn't perform
it. Be confident in God.

July 8

You were fashioned
to endure, designed
to win, and created to
withstand.

You have no reason to be afraid or intimidated by situations that stare at you, trying to appear bigger, better, larger, or stronger. God reminded Ezekiel that He made us harder than flint and told Him not to be dismayed by the way that people look at him (Ezekiel 3:9).

July 9

> If God promised it, He
> doesn't need your help
> to perform it.

God is very clear about what He says and
what He promises. He is equally clear about
His ability to fulfill His word.

When you allow the "who I shall be" to show up more than the "who I used to be," miracles happen.

How you handle this moment – this very moment – could affect the rest your life.

When you stay in faith, favor will show up. Look for it, and when it shows up, don't mistake it for anything else.

God's presence used to manifest as a cloud. To some, it could have been mistaken as the threat of a rainstorm. Be open to favor, no matter how it shows up!

If you're not willing to
help others find their
destiny, your destiny
may never find you.

July 14

There is no need
to look for a huge
spotlight, when a small
match-light is all you
need.

There is a light within you, and no matter
how small it may be, it still has the power to
pierce the darkness. That one small light in
you is enough to set the world on fire.

Don't worry about not being able to get to God because God knows how to get to you!

The difference between
ignorance and a lie
is that ignorance is
curable and can be
forgiven pretty quickly.

It's better to seem ignorant than be proven as a liar. Don't feel as though you must have an answer just because someone asks you a question. It's okay to say, "I don't know."

July 17

It does us no good to
win the battle for our
pride, if we lose the
battle for our souls.

Revenge and retaliation are about pride.
Let's pick the right battle – souls first.

People won't TRAVEL WITH you if they can't TRUST IN you.

With all that you might offer or possess, before you expect people to trail you, give them a reason to trust you.

Make people matter. Be kind – humankind.

Without a clean heart,
a clean building means
nothing to God.

Maintain your
connection to God –
even in an area where
the signal is weak.

If you really want to impress God with your giving, give Him your heart.

You will never see the
beauty in God's word,
until you open your
eyes … and the pages.

The congruence and parallelism of God's
word is easily seen if we would only read it.

July 24

Skip rope, not church.

I'm committed to
pleasing God because
God is committed to
blessing me.

Even when people are conflicted, God
is very clear about His intentions regarding
you. God is committed to seeing us from one
victory to another. Let this be your testimony
today: "I'm committed to please God and
whatever it takes, I'm all in.

For every one funeral
you must attend, go to
two parties you'd like
to attend.

When others try to "write" you off, let God "right" you back in. Cash-in your "redemption chips" as often as possible.

Righteousness means something to God; and He will not let your righteousness go unrewarded. Righteousness is what justifies you in the sight of God.

July 28

> Your life is filled
> with the promise
> that someone else is
> anticipating.

Their garden might never grow if you don't fill your pot with water. They may never get it, if you don't release it. Do your part, so that others might live, just as others have done their part so that you might live.

Without a heart and humility, you may never capture the ear of God.

God heard Daniel as soon as he surrendered his heart and humbled himself (Daniel 10:12). He's not the kind of God who would do it for Daniel without doing it for us.

Your reputation runs
faster than your legs.

Live so that you can
help bring Christ in
the time of crisis.

Let's live so that people can call on us to help jump-start their batteries when they are dying. How we live matters! There was a woman named Tabitha who lived in Joppa. When she died, the people called for Peter (Acts 9:36-38). Be "Peter" in somebody's life.

The ripples that you create today might be the same ones that drown you tomorrow.

Every bad thing that
stayed out is a result
of the good things that
God allowed in.

God knows how to fill your cup, your basket, your heart, and your life with GOOD THINGS.

Every time you tell God "Thank you," He has a miraculous way of saying, "You're welcome."

When you are kind
enough to give God
your gratitude, He is
powerful enough to
give you His favor. You
might want to be kind
to God!

Trust God in the dark
just as much as you
trust Him in the light.

It's easy to trust God when we see Him moving, but during those dark moments when we can't see Him, feel Him, or hear Him; the least we should do is to trust Him.

Don't hold God hostage for something that He didn't promise.

God never promised a life without disappointment or heartache. He never promised that we wouldn't sometimes get upset with Him, but what He promised was that whatever we go through, He would go through it with us.

Sometimes God will answer a prayer FOR you; other times He will answer a prayer THROUGH you. Be the answer to someone's prayer.

If you can't feed others
as you follow, go to
the end of the line so
no one will have to
follow you.

Your attitude about what you give is more important that the size of your gift.

Don't let someone else's
distraction delay your
deliverance.

There was a man with a withered hand
sitting in a synagogue, and rather than letting
Jesus focus on healing the man, the Pharisees
wanted to challenge Him about performing
miracles on the Sabbath (Matthew 12:10).

Stop staring at the
questions, and start
looking for the
answers.

You don't get credit just for being religious, but you do get credit for having a relationship.

There is no reward in just believing because even the demons believe (James 2:19).

Until you learn to forgive like Christ, you have not learned to forgive at all. Forgive without conditions!

Go ahead and ask God; someone else might be waiting for the answer too.

Don't worship just so God can hear you, but worship so that you can hear God.

God will not only redeem your time, but He will also redeem your tears. He knows how to give you blessings that are worth every tear that you have ever shed.

The world was never intended to be without light; and neither were we. We were designed to always carry and reflect the light of God.

Don't get distracted by
the moment; focus on
the mission.

If I'm going to choose
the wrong seat, I'd
rather it be one of
humility rather than
one of honor. There
is no need for God
to exalt you if you're
going to exalt yourself.

Even if the place
and the process
are unfamiliar, the
provider is always the
same.

When you need
directions, stop
ignoring the signs.

If you haven't found
God to be faithful, then
you haven't been with
Him long enough.

If you lift His name,
He'll lift your life.

God will never push
you in a swimming
pool without first
teaching you how to
swim.

Just because you are forgiven, that doesn't mean that you won't sometimes have to still deal with the consequences.

Blessings are not based on WHAT you give but WHERE you give them from.

Your small brushstroke is adding to the big picture that God is painting for somebody else's life. Choose your colors carefully.

Something you do
today is going to get
God's attention, so be
very careful because
He might just respond.

I would rather have God marvel at me rather than menace at me. In Luke 7:9, Jesus marveled and commented on the faith of the Roman centurion.

When you can't call anybody else to be your witness, you should be able to call your character and your reputation.

August 30

You can't be like Christ
unless you BEHAVE
like Christ.

243

If you remember the
promises FOR your life,
you will avoid some of
the pitfalls IN your life.

Life peels off the layers
and leaves us naked;
but Christ shed His
blood so we could
always be covered.

While you're rejoicing
at what God has done
for you, don't forget
to rejoice at what He's
done for others.

The same God who
showed up for Moses
wants to show up
for you.

The enemy is like a virus. He never comes when you are at your strongest, but he comes when your resistance is down.

God won't lead you through a battle and then not take care of your scars.

There's no need to praise in public if you can't worship in private.

I'd rather go to heaven with only what I need than go to hell with all that I want.

If my eyes cause me to disobey God, I'd rather go to heaven blind than go hell with sight.

Man's attention might be what you want, but God's attention is what you need.

It's better to make a joyful noise before God and keep silent before men than to make a noise before men and keep silent before God.

If you want sinners
to change their ways,
don't condemn them;
commune with them.

Jesus ate with sinners, and it changed their lives.

When I want sympathy, I complain; when I want strength, I commune. It's all about HOW you say what you say.

September 11

If you ever start
counting your
blessings, you probably
will never stop.

September 12

> Don't get trapped by
> what you hold, but set
> yourself free by what
> you release.

Release the thoughts that come to detain, disconcert, dissuade, demean, deter, and distract you. Be transformed [from bondage to freedom] by the renewing of your mind (Romans 12:2).

September 13

God will never abort
His plan for me, just
because I stopped
dreaming.

He would not have written a plan but then
fail to carry it out. He is the author AND the
finisher (Hebrews 12:2).

If you're not going to
help construct, then
don't bother to critique.

It might not turn out like you want it, but it WILL turn out. God won't leave you alone in it.

Don't just double your
pleasure, but triple
your treasure.

While you're enjoying life take some time to invest in yourself. Partner with people. Explore your dreams. Expand your network. Do something new. Take a chance. Make God glad about the things that He gave you.

If you guard your faith,
God will guard your
future.

September 18

Don't let your mind
talk you out of your
miracle.

Don't overthink the small promptings and leadings of God.

God looks at me
because of my faith,
but He answers
me because of my
obedience.

Life, like a good set
of tires, requires
alignment and balance.

Get what you need
from God quickly, and
you'll enjoy it a lot
longer.

Job 22:21 reminds us to agree with God quickly and good will come to you.

One of the worst things that you could ever steal from a child is his laughter.

Life is like a gym
where we "pull-up"
ourselves and
"push-up" our brothers
and sisters.

September 24

> Learn to think and live
> outside the box before
> you are finally placed
> in a box.

You'll be in a box soon enough one day, but while you are alive, as long as you don't hurt anybody else or harm yourself, tap into your God-given creativity as often as you can.

If we would acknowledge and thank God when it seems to matter the least, He will be there when it matters the most.

You don't have to become a zealot or a fanatic, but life goes better with God in it. Make God matter.

If we can learn to
control our mouths,
then we might have a
shot at controlling our
emotions. Everything
doesn't have to
come out.

God is an
impossibility-handler.

Reciprocity is paramount in relationships. Live in Christ and let Christ live in you.

You can't fix yourself if you're always fighting others. Stop fighting and start fixing.

Gossiping with one group gets your name inserted on the subject line of another group.

Stop trying to be right all of the time and try to be righteous some of the time.

We don't have to be right all the time, but let's get the righteous piece right.

> Be honest – in love and in hate.

When it comes to the things that you like and the things that you don't like, just TELL THE TRUTH.

Allow people to hate
what you love and love
what you hate. Broaden
your perspective.

Don't assume that everyone else's
experiences are like yours.

On the quest to your individual promised land, devote more of your attention to the opportunities, not the obstacles. Do the work, not the worrying!

One good person by
your side can be worth
more than a whole
army in your face.

Jeremiah had a king (Zedekiah) and
presumably the whole nation in his face, but
it didn't matter because God was by his side
(Jeremiah 32:6-9).

You will never know
peace until you drain
the toxicity from your
life.

Peace is like a stream of pure water.
Toxicity is like motor oil drained from a car.
The two were never intended to occupy the
same space.

Friends who fumble
by mistake might get
resuscitated; but those
who foul on purpose
might get euthanized.

It's easier to forgive people if they hurt you
by mistake or if they had good intentions.
However, purposefully contaminating a
relationship creates a huge gulf that human
forgiveness doesn't always span.

> Hurt and frustration
> are sometimes the tools
> that God uses to scrape
> away the rust, but He
> still manages to leave
> you shiny.

We don't realize that many times, we are walking around as precious metal with rust deposits that cling to us as a result of being exposed to life and its elements. It becomes so easy for us to accept the rust as a part of our norm. Because rust clings and doesn't want to let go, it takes a strong instrument and a precise tool to discern between the rust and the metal. God has the right tools to get the job done.

Take the breaks that
life allows, but learn
to step away without
disconnecting.

It's quite possible and probable that we
all need to step away from family, friends,
church, or work from time to time. People get
away and go on vacation all the time. That
doesn't mean they are any less committed to
a cause just because they stepped away. Step
away, but don't stay away.

Sometimes it's best not
to get in the way of the
tides of life.

Let the rivers flow where they may, and if you can't appreciate what's going on, just shift positions and get a new perspective.

The ultimate goal in life is not to "obtain and acquire;" the ultimate goal is to "live and lead."

Live a life that is pleasing to God, and lead others to Christ.

If you have a point
to prove, don't argue;
testify instead.

Extend grace
without judgment,
mercy without self-
righteousness, and
forgiveness without
condemnation.

Trusting in riches
without trusting in
God might make you
happy, but it won't
make you complete.

Don't get paralyzed
just because you don't
know the plan; keep
marching, even in the
face of uncertainty.

The women who went to the graveyard to
anoint the body of Jesus had no idea how they
would roll away the stone and get inside tomb
(Mark 16:3). They had uncertainty, but they
kept marching.

God wants to hear from you again!

Even though Peter denied Christ, it must have been comforting for him to know that Christ wanted to see him again. When the women discovered that the tomb was empty and that the stoned had been rolled away, the angel told the women to go and tell the disciples – and specifically named Peter – that the Lord was waiting to see them in Galilee (Mark 16:7).

God sees you coming,
even if everyone else
has closed the door.

Let's pray and plan a "welcome back" party for all the prodigal sons and daughters in our lives. Let's pray that they too will say: "I'm so thankful that GOD SAW ME COMING!"

God would have never called you good, if "good" couldn't come from you. God believes in you.

It's chilling and sobering to realize that we have something in common with criminals. Jesus came for us, but He came for them too.

Give God your RSVP
before it's too late.

Life gives us many options; death offers us only two.

In life we get to start over; but in death we can't un-do.

God is not duplicitous. He does not talk out of both sides of His mouth.

God knows what He's thinking; and He has not changed His mind concerning His blessings for your life.

It takes only one dirty
hand to make a clean
thing dirty. Don't
contaminate the things,
places, or people
of God.

Stop looking FOR the revelation; and look AT the manifestation.

God reveals Himself every day – through nature and through His creation. The Apostle Paul said God has given us a revelation of who He is through His creation, so we have no excuse not to believe in God (Romans 1:20). We don't need a deeper revelation of God; we just need to open our eyes and behold the manifestation!

Whenever you get the
privilege to "have,"
you also get the
responsibility to "do."

God handles guilt
much better than we
do. He keeps it and
offers us grace instead.

When the probability
of offending God
means more than the
possibility of receiving
forgiveness, we are
more inclined to do
what's right.

Some people sin because offending God
means very little to them.

God has always known
you, even before you
knew what it meant to
be known.

You are not a stranger to God. Rest assured
that He knows exactly who you are.

Christ has the right
to condemn us, but
instead He prays.
We have the need to
pray but instead we
condemn.

God never created
anything or anybody
that is powerful
enough to cause Him
NOT to love us.

Nothing and no one has ever been – nor
will ever be – powerful enough to prevent
God from loving you.

We are victorious –
not because of our
behavior, but – because
of our belief.

Our relationship with Christ makes us "more than conquerors through him that loved us" (Romans 8:37).

I don't worry about not knowing the details of the story of my life, as long as I know the author … and the finisher.

We satisfy our debt
to God, partly by
loving our fellow man
(Romans 13:8).

Don't argue with people about what you believe. Just tell them that "God said it," and then leave them to argue with God.

We have access to the greatest part of God's plan - JESUS CHRIST!

Jesus is not only the king who rules, but He is the high priest who intercedes.

He still sits at the right hand of the Father, as the exalted Savior; yet He pleads our case.

> If Jesus built it and left
> you with it, take care
> of it.

He's trusting us to be good stewards of His church, His people, and His world.

Take off the mask.
God already SEES
and KNOWS
EVERYTHING!

Sing, even if you can't hit the notes. Call it a "new song" (Psalm 96:1).

Don't play "Hide and Seek" with what God said. If you're not holding up the gospel, you're hiding it.

The responsibility of the believer is to share the gospel with ALL people (Psalm 96:3), especially those who don't believe.

Promote the gospel;
don't pervert it
(Galatians 1:7).

It's not rude to talk
while others are
talking, if you're
talking to God.

Love is more than a noun!

Trust the reciprocity
of relationships. If we
abide in Christ, He will
abide in us (John 15:4).

Give God the hammer
and just pass Him the
nails. God is able to
build a better life for you
than you can build for
yourself. He designed
the blueprint for your
life, so let him lead.

Discern your position in God's plan for
our life. Sometimes you may have a leading
role; other times, you just need to provide
support. God allows us to participate in the
construction, but He's the master builder.
"Except the Lord build the house, they labour
in vain that build it" (Psalm 127:1). It will last
longer if we just let God build it.

We've got the hand of God and the heart of God over our lives.

He protects us with His rod; He rescues us with his staff; and He showers us with goodness and mercy.

Stop using God's word as a battering ram.

You can't use God's word to find fault, yet not offer hope; and you can't stand in judgment without extending grace.

My greatest victories
are never over people
but over predicaments
and possibilities.

If we are going to
be overcomers, let's
overcome. If we are
going to be winners,
let's win. If we are
going to be believers,
let's believe.

If you give God a house, He will give you a kingdom.

If you COME CLEAN
with God, God will
COME THROUGH
for you.

Everything that God gives you makes you attractive to the enemy.

Be discerning and discriminating when sharing your gifts. Exploitation and manipulation are very real.

Your value to God has less to do with how important you are and more to do with how importunate you are.

My faith has an
answer – even when
my intellect doesn't.

Hatred on any level is hatred on every level. Love on restricted levels is love on no level.

If we don't matter
to anybody else, we
matter … to God.

We are the reflection of God's masterful work. We have the breath of the Creator of the world inside us.

Where you failed
could be the same
place where you will
flourish.

Sometimes casting your net in the same waters will yield different results when your faith and perspective are different.

It's lonely at the top, only for those persons who are constantly pushing down others. There's enough room at the top for all of us.

Before you try to speak FOR God, make sure you speak TO God.

A green apple in your mouth won't leave a sour taste in my mouth.

Your experiences are uniquely yours; and if by chance we share similar experiences, it's okay to have different outcomes. Learn how to independently develop your own thoughts, opinions, and ideas.

Some victories are won
not because of WHAT
you have, but because
of HOW you use what
you have.

December 1

> The same way we want Jesus to remember us, He wants us to remember Him.

It is our hope that He remembers us ALL day EVERY day. When He communed with the disciples, He urged them: "remember me" (1 Corinthians 11:24-26). Let's celebrate Him as often as we can.

If it can't help heal me, I can't hold it.

There is no reason to hold on to things that don't contribute to your healing or growth. If medicine, medical equipment, or medical professionals were not effective in bringing about healing, chances are we would look for viable alternatives. It may be wise to apply this behavior to the people, principles, and practices that impact our peace of mind and sense of well-being.

If you didn't do it, don't
carry the crown or the
cross.

Don't just pray so that God will hear you, but also pray so that the enemy will hear you - and tremble.

Sometimes, you've got to put the enemy on notice that his attempt to derail God's plan for your life is futile and in vain.

Even when your life is on fire, you can still fellowship with God. God does not forsake us just because the fiery trials get hotter.

Strive to strike a balance between belief and behavior. Think first! Think second! Do third!

If you stop insulting
your integrity and
diminishing your
dignity, maybe others
will stop challenging
you to compromise
your character.

Live like the hen who never knows what's inside her egg. Wait, incubate, and then celebrate.

The thing that God
does for you today
will get you through
tomorrow.

You are never
expected to give what
you haven't been
empowered to get.
Know what's in your
arsenal.

Sometimes God gives you the GIFT. Other times He gives you the ABILITY to get the gift.

The mercy of God will always baffle the carnal mind.

There is a place for
those who do the will
of God, and there is
a place for those who
do not.

While you're being "real" and "transparent," don't forget to "be holy."

Instead of letting
trouble defeat you,
allow it to develop you.

What you sow today
will show tomorrow; so
be kind to creation.

When God asks a
questions, it's not for
His benefit but for
yours. He already
knows the answer.

Shun disobedience; it makes you look naked and stupid.

When God asked Adam, "Where are you," Adam said that he had hidden because he was naked (Genesis 3:10). News alert: Adam had ALWAYS been naked but he had not hidden before.

December 18

Internal conflict: Just
because you carry it,
that doesn't mean you
have to give birth to it.

It's better to resolve it than to release it.

It does us no good to
have a full stomach
and an empty soul.

Just because you GOT THROUGH IT, that doesn't mean you GOT AWAY WITH IT! Look for the summons and the subpoena any day now.

Life is like math. When the numbers don't add up, look at the signs!

7 + 2=9
7 - 2=5
7 x 2=14
7 ÷ 2=3.5

> God will never trust
> me with the fish in the
> boat if He can't trust
> me with the nets on
> the shore.

When Jesus called the disciples, it was apparent that not only did they appreciate the promise of the boat, but they also understood the preparation on the dock.

It's not always about what you GET; sometimes what really matters is what you KEEP.

December 24

Stop looking for
revenge and start
looking for rewards!

Just because it's
rational, that doesn't
make it right.

There are no neutral
people in your life.
They are either positive
or negative, and sooner
or later their energy
will empower you or
impede you.

If you're not practicing self-improvement, you're practicing suicide.

Learning should not just be a portion of your life, but it should be a practice in your life. Always strive to improve and sharpen yourself by learning something. A sharp axe will chop more trees.

December 28

God's way of getting
out of it is better than
our way of staying in it.

Whenever God gives
you somebody that
becomes a priority in
your life, make sure
that God is a priority
in their life.

With all of our spiritual depth and profundity, there are still times when our discernment might be off. That's a reminder that we are still human.

The priest Eli read Hannah's lips as she prayed, and he surmised that she was drunk; but she was far from drunk. She had not had anything to drink. Her heart was broken and her soul was wounded (1 Samuel 1:12-16).

There's no expiration
date on God's ability to
answer prayers.

Just when it looks like you've run out of
time, God will either extend the deadline; or
He will reset the clock.

Bonus Quotes

If you ever find yourself in need of an extra lift for your day, or if you are ever in need of a healthy conversation starter, take a look at these bonus quotes.

- *God plays fair, but I wouldn't suggest toying around with Him.*

- *He didn't create me to consume me, so instead He cloaks me.*

- *It doesn't always make sense to trust God; but don't follow because of sense; follow because of faith.*

- *God specializes in defying logic. He will use the foolish things to confound the wise (1 Corinthians 1:27).*

- *Your words will live, even when you have died.*

- *A lie is what happens when you use both sides of your mouth.*

- *Don't be concerned when you're not the guest of honor; just be thankful you got an invitation.*

- *It's better to accept God's plan than to expect Him to accept yours.*

๛ You can't talk about the gift in His hand without talking about the gift in His heart. "For God so loved the world that he gave …" (John 3:16).

๛ It's not God's house if He never shows up; and it's not God's heart if He was never invited.

๛ God is not auditioning for His own role, but He can always use a few stagehands.

๛ When God heals, there is no relapse!

๛ While you are looking for a healing, God might be planning a resurrection. Let God do it His way. Let Him show you what a real miracle looks like.

๛ No one has the ability to ruin your day except for the one who runs your day.

๛ Work WITH God, not AGAINST Him.

๛ Your mouth is like a motor. It will either move you or immobilize you.

๛ Meditate on the promise not on the problem.

๛ My future is in God's hands because my hands can barely hold my present.

๛ Assumptions and inferences will cripple you until you get the courage to search for answers. Just ask the question.

- *If you desire something that's not worth repeating in prayer, it's probably not worth asking for the first time.*

- *Every valley of defeat is an experience at God's feet; lie there, and watch Him trample the enemies of your soul.*

- *The very THOUGHTS OF GOD are so powerful that they can leap out of the CREVICES OF HIS IMAGINATION and create a CANVAS OF REALITY.*

Made in the USA
Middletown, DE
27 June 2020

11400960R00227